FIRST LADY SUITE

A MUSICAL BY
MICHAEL JOHN LaCHIUSA

DRAMATISTS
PLAY SERVICE
INC.

FIRST LADY SUITE
Copyright © 1995, Michael John LaChiusa

All Rights Reserved

FIRST LADY SUITE is fully protected under the copyright laws of the United States of America, and of all countries covered by the International Copyright Union (including the Dominion of Canada and the rest of the British Commonwealth), and of all countries covered by the Pan-American Copyright Convention, the Universal Copyright Convention, the Berne Convention, and of all countries with which the United States has reciprocal copyright relations. No part of this publication may be reproduced in any form by any means (electronic, mechanical, photocopying, recording, or otherwise), or stored in any retrieval system in any way (electronic or mechanical) without written permission of the publisher.

The English language stock and amateur stage performance rights in the United States, its territories, possessions and Canada for FIRST LADY SUITE are controlled exclusively by Dramatists Play Service, 440 Park Avenue South, New York, NY 10016. **No professional or nonprofessional performance of the Play(s) may be given without obtaining in advance the written permission of Dramatists Play Service and paying the requisite fee.**

All other rights, including without limitation motion picture, recitation, lecturing, public reading, radio broadcasting, television, video or sound recording, and the rights of translation into foreign languages are strictly reserved.

Inquiries concerning all other rights should be addressed to Creative Artists Agency, 405 Lexington Avenue, 19th Floor, New York, NY 10174. Attn: George Lane.

NOTE ON BILLING

Anyone receiving permission to produce FIRST LADY SUITE is required to give credit to the Author as sole and exclusive Author of the Play(s) on the title page of all programs distributed in connection with performances of the Play(s) and in all instances in which the title of the Play(s) appears, including printed or digital materials for advertising, publicizing or otherwise exploiting the Play(s) and/or a production thereof. The name of the Author must appear on a separate line, in which no other name appears, immediately beneath the title and in size of type equal to 50% of the size of the largest, most prominent letter used for the title of the Play(s). No person, firm or entity may receive credit larger or more prominent than the Author. The following acknowledgments must appear on the title page in all programs distributed in connection with performances of the Play(s):

Original New York Production by
The New York Shakespeare Festival

OVER TEXAS and WHERE'S MAMIE were originally developed by the Ensemble Studio Theatre, Curt Dempster, Artistic Director; Dominick Balletta, Managing Director; Kate Baggott, Producer.

TABLE OF CONTENTS

OVER TEXAS 7

WHERE'S MAMIE? 29

OLIO 53

ELEANOR SLEEPS HERE 59

FIRST LADY SUITE was produced by New York Shakespeare Festival (George C. Wolfe, Artistic Director), in New York City, in December, 1993. It was directed by Kirsten Sanderson; the set design was by Derek McLane; the costume design was by Tom Broecker; the lighting design was by Brian MacDevitt; the musical direction was by Alan Johnson; the choreography was by Janet Bogardus and the production stage manager was Liz Small. The cast was as follows:

OVER TEXAS
EVELYN LINCOLN .... Carolann Page
MARY GALLAGHER .... Debra Stricklin
A PRESIDENTIAL AIDE .... David Wasson
THE FIRST LADY (Jacqueline Bouvier Kennedy) .... Maureen Moore
LADY BIRD JOHNSON .... Alice Playten

WHERE'S MAMIE?
MAMIE EISENHOWER .... Alice Playten
MARIAN ANDERSON ....Priscilla Baskerville
IKE (Dwight D. Eisenhower) .... David Wasson
IKE'S CHAUFFEUR .... Debra Stricklin

OLIO
BESS TRUMAN .... David Wasson
MARGARET TRUMAN .... Debra Stricklin

ELEANOR SLEEPS HERE
ELEANOR ROOSEVELT .... Carolann Page
HICK (Lorena Hickok) .... Carol Woods
AMELIA EARHART .... Maureen Moore

OVER TEXAS

Characters:
EVELYN LINCOLN (Personal Secretary to President John F. Kennedy)
MARY GALLAGHER (Personal Secretary to the First Lady)
A PRESIDENTIAL AIDE
THE FIRST LADY (Jacqueline Bouvier Kennedy)
LADY BIRD JOHNSON

On board Air Force One, en route from Fort Worth to Love Field, Dallas, Texas. November 22, 1963.

WHERE'S MAMIE?

Characters:
MAMIE (Mary Geneva Doud Eisenhower)
MARIAN ANDERSON
IKE (Dwight D. Eisenhower)
IKE'S CHAUFFEUR (Kay Summersby)

Ike and Mamie Eisenhower's bedroom, the White House. 1957.

OLIO

Characters:
BESS TRUMAN
MARGARET TRUMAN

A luncheon for Christian Democratic mothers and daughters. 1950.

ELEANOR SLEEPS HERE

Characters:
ELEANOR ROOSEVELT
HICK (Lorena Hickok)
AMELIA EARHART

Interior of Amelia Earhart's Lockheed Electra. Night. 1936.

OVER TEXAS

OVER TEXAS

Air Force One. Staff Cabin. 1963. Evelyn Lincoln is seated, typing. After a moment, Mary Gallagher joins her.

MARY.
    ALWAYS SOMETHING.
    FIRST THE COMBS.
    THEN THE HAT.
    YOU'D THINK THE WORLD
    WAS COMING TO AN END
    OVER COMBS.
    AND A HAT.
    ALWAYS SOMETHING WRONG.
    NEVER SOMETHING RIGHT.
    THE COMBS.
    THE HAT.
    THE HEM.
    THE STITCH.
    WHAT.
    WHERE.
    WHEN.
    WHICH.
    ALWAYS SOMETHING WITH *HER.*
    I'M POOPED ...
    ALWAYS SOMETHING.

EVELYN.
    SHE LIKES TO LOOK NICE.

MARY. *(Displaying a kit of needle and thread.)*
    THEY HAVE LITTLE SEWING KITS
    ON AIR FORCE ONE—
    CAN YOU IMAGINE?
    THEY HAVE EVERYTHING

ON AIR FORCE ONE.
... WHAT YOU WORKING ON, EVELYN?

EVELYN.
MEMOS FOR THE CHIEF.
HIS SPEECH.
AT THE TRADE MART.
(Looking up, seriously.)
THEY'RE EXPECTING DEMONSTRATIONS.

MARY.
... LOOKS PRETTY WET OUT THERE.
... SHE'LL PROB'LY NEED HER COAT.
(A pause.)
I BET THAT TOM KITTEN MISSES ME.
I BET HE'S CHEWING UP THE HOUSE.
I BET HE'S SULKING IN HIS CHAIR,
SCRATCHING AT HIS HEAD,
"WHEN'S SHE COMING HOME?"
"WHEN'LL I GET FED?"
(A pause.)
I BET THAT TOM KITTEN MISSES ME.
I BET HE'S POOPING ON THE RUG.
AND HERE I AM:
FLYING OVER TEXAS.
HERE I AM:
AND TICKLED TO BE,
WHO'D'VE THUNK
I'D BE FLYING OVER TEXAS
ON A PLANE WITH THE PRESIDENT—
A REAL V.I.P.!
I BET THAT TOM KITTEN ENVIES ME.
I BET HE'S RAISING HOLY HECK.
I BET HE'S THINKING THAT I'VE LEFT
LEAVING HIM FOR DEAD.
"WHEN'S SHE COMING HOME?"
"WHEN'LL I GET FED?"
HUNGRY, WHINEY, LAZY, FAT;
I ALMOST MISS THAT CRAZY CAT

>   BUT HERE I SIT
>   ON A PLANE WITH THE PRESIDENT.
>   MILES IN THE SKY.
>   I BET THAT TOM KITTEN MISSES ME.
>   I BET HE'S WISHING HE COULD
>   FLY …

EVELYN.
>   IT'S NICE TO GET AWAY
>   FROM THE DESK FOR A FEW DAYS.

MARY.
>   OH YES INDEEDY!
>   IT'S AN ADVENTURE
>   SURE!
>   I LOVE IT!
>   *SHE* DOESN'T.

EVELYN.
>   CAMPAIGNING CAN BE HARD.

MARY.
>   FOR *HER* IT IS …
>   SHE SMOKED A WHOLE PACK OF SALEMS.

EVELYN.
>   SHE'S BEEN THROUGH SO MUCH.

MARY.
>   SHE'S NERVOUS.
>   THE CHIEF IS NERVOUS.
>   EVERYONE IS NERVOUS.
>   I'M NOT.
>   I'M JUST POOPED.

(A Presidential Aide enters with a tea tray.)

AIDE.
>   LADIES?
>   TEA?

MARY.

    Oh, yes! Thank you!

(The Aide exits.)

    HOW NICE...!
    THIS IS NICE.
    TEA ON AIR FORCE ONE.
    CAN YOU IMAGINE?
    ... OF COURSE YOU CAN.
    THE PRESIDENT TAKES YOU EVERYWHERE.
    I DON'T GO ANYWHERE
    WITH *HER.*
    ... She won't let me ride in the motorcade. I have to go on ahead to the hotel and unpack.

EVELYN.

    THEY'RE EXPECTING DEMONSTRATIONS.

MARY. *(Thinking Evelyn means a parade or something festive.)*
    I *know.*
(Raising her teacup.)
    TO THE CHIEF.

EVELYN.

    TO FOUR MORE YEARS.

(They toast teacups. Evelyn drinks.)

MARY.

    There's something floating in mine ...

(She watches Evelyn drink. Evelyn truly enjoys her tea.)

EVELYN.

    This is good.

(Mary picks at whatever is floating in her teacup.)

MARY.

    FOUR MORE YEARS.
    ANSWERING HER PHONES.

SORTING OUT HER BILLS.
FOUR MORE YEARS.
PICKING UP HER HATS.
PICKING OUT HER GLOVES.
SLOWLY GOING BATS
ADDING UP HER BILLS.
MAKING SURE HER DAIQUIRIS ARE MADE.
"NOT TOO SWEET."
"NOT TOO SWEET."
MAKING SURE HER CREDITORS ARE PAID.
"DON'T TELL JACK."
"DON'T TELL JACK."
FOUR MORE YEARS
WAITING FOR HER CALL.
LEAPING TO HER DOOR.
HEARING HER COMPLAIN.
WONDERING: WHAT FOR?

MARY. *(To herself.)*
FOUR MORE YEARS:
THIS IS NOT A LIFE,
SORTING OUT HER BILLS.
FOUR MORE YEARS:
MAYBE I SHOULD QUIT.
WOULDN'T SHE BE PEEVED?
IF I'D EVER QUIT
WHO WOULD SORT HER BILLS?

I WAKE UP MY HEAD BEGINS
TO THROB —

— FOR THE CHIEF.

— EVERYDAY.
WHAT IS THE DESCRIPTION
OF MY JOB?

EVELYN. *(To herself.)*
FOUR MORE YEARS
ANSWERING HIS PHONES,
WAITING FOR HIS VOICE.
FOUR MORE YEARS:
HOPING THAT HE SMILES,

KNOWING WHEN HE'S
HAPPY ...

IT'S FOR JACK.

— ALL FOR HIM.

    — LOTS OF GRIEF.

    — EVERYDAY
WAITING FOR HER VOICE,
RUNNING TO HER DESK,
ALL THE ENDLESS NOTES,
ALL THE ENDLESS GRIEF,
HELPING HER —

KNOWING HER —

BEING THERE —

ALWAYS THERE,
WONDERING:
COULD I GO BACK?

FOR
FOUR MORE YEARS
WITH JACKIE —
(They look at each other and smile.)
    — AND JACK ...
(The Aide re-enters.)

    — LOTS OF WORK.

    — SO MUCH WORK.

WAITING FOR HIS VOICE,
WAITING FOR HIS SMILE,
WAITING FOR HIS LAUGH,
WAITING FOR HIS WORD,

    — HELPING HIM ...

    — KNOWING HIM ...

    — BEING THERE ...

    — I HAVE TO GO BACK
FOR
FOUR MORE YEARS
WITH JACKIE —

    — AND JACK ...

AIDE.

    We'll be landing in eight minutes.
    LADIES.

MARY.

    If Mrs. Kennedy needs me I'll be *right here.*

AIDE.

    I'm sorry.... Who are you?

MARY.

    Mary Gallagher.

EVELYN.

    Mrs. Kennedy's secretary.

MARY.

    Jackie's secretary.

AIDE.

    Yes, Mary Gallagher. Thank you, Mrs. Lincoln.
(The Aide exits.)

MARY.

    OH! THIS IS FUNNY:
    CAROLINE COMES INTO MY OFFICE
    NOT TOO LONG AGO —
    DID I TELL YOU THIS?
    ANYWAY.
    SHE ASKS ME IF I HAVE
    THE CHICKEN POX.
    I SAY, OF COURSE, I DON'T HAVE
    THE CHICKEN POX.
    I'VE NEVER EVER HAD
    THE CHICKEN POX.
    AND CAROLINE SAYS:
    — THIS IS SO FUNNY! —
    CAROLINE SAYS:
    "THEN I'LL HUG YOU AND GIVE YOU
    MY CHICKEN POX!"
    ...! DID I TELL YOU THIS?

EVELYN.

    Yes.

MARY.

    THOSE KIDS ...

EVELYN.

    HE'S A GOOD DADDY.
    THE CHIEF.

MARY.
>OH YES, INDEEDY.
>BUT *HER.*
>NEVER CEASES TO SURPRISE ME.

EVELYN.
>EVERYDAY IT'S SOMETHING NEW.

MARY.
>TIME FOR A KITTY CAT NAP.
>I'LL JUST CLOSE MY EYES.
>SHE'LL PROB'LY WANT ME.
>THE MINUTE THAT I CLOSE MY EYES
>SHE'LL WANT ME.
>NEVER FAILS.
>ALWAYS SOMETHING.

EVELYN.
>I BETTER GET THIS TO THE CHIEF.

MARY.
>I DON'T KNOW ...
>I BET THAT TOM KITTEN MISSES ME.

(Evelyn exits.)
>MAYBE NOT ...
>I DON'T KNOW ...

(Mary nods off. The First Lady enters. She wears a raspberry pink Chanel suit with blue accents. She sits next to Mary. Her hat and gloves are in her lap.)

FIRST LADY.
>... How is Tom Kitten, Mary?

MARY. *(Sleepy.)*
>Fine ...

FIRST LADY.
>WE CAN'T HAVE CATS IN THE WHITE HOUSE.

MARY.
> I know …

FIRST LADY.
> HE HAS A NICE HOME WITH YOU.

MARY.
> I said he was fine.

FIRST LADY.
> THE PRESIDENT GAVE TOM KITTEN TO YOU.

MARY.
> Look, I'm pooped. See … *(Demonstrates.)* I'm pooped!

FIRST LADY.
> WHERE'S MY HAT?

MARY.
> There. You're holding it.

FIRST LADY.
> WHERE ARE MY GLOVES?

MARY.
> In your hands.

FIRST LADY.
> IT'S THE DETAILS THAT COUNT.

MARY.
> I want to sleep. Why can't you let me sleep?

(Lady Bird Johnson enters. She pauses a moment by the First Lady and Mary.)

LADY BIRD.
> LADIES.

FIRST LADY.
    Oh! Lady Bird. How does it feel to be back in your home state?

LADY BIRD.
    Yes.
(Lady Bird exits.)

FIRST LADY.
    DO YOU THINK I'LL NEED MY COAT
    IN DALLAS?

MARY.
    I don't know.

FIRST LADY.
    WHERE'S MY HAT?

MARY.
    I don't care.

FIRST LADY.
    WHERE ARE MY GLOVES?

MARY.
    I DON'T CARE!
    IN YOUR HANDS!
    RIGHT THERE!
    IN YOUR HANDS!

FIRST LADY.
    Don't tell Jack ...

MARY.
    WHAT DO YOU WANT?
    FOUR YEARS:
    ANSWERING YOUR PHONES.
    TYPING UP YOUR NOTES.
    SORTING OUT YOUR BILLS.
    HEARING YOU COMPLAIN —

A THOUSAND YEARS!
YOU WON'T EVEN LET ME RIDE
IN THE MOTORCADE.

FIRST LADY.
THERE'S SO MUCH WORK TO BE DONE —

MARY.
— I WANT MY FAMILY!
I WANT VACATIONS!
I WANT MORE.
I WANT—

FIRST LADY.
What, Mary?

MARY. *(Letting her have it.)*
I WANT
TO NEVER HEAR YOUR VOICE AGAIN!
I WANT
TO NEVER SEE YOUR FACE AGAIN!
OR YOUR HAT!
OR YOUR GLOVES!
I NEVER THOUGHT MY LIFE
WOULD BE LIKE THIS!

FIRST LADY.
Yes! That's what it is!! Yes, Mary! That's what it is…!

MARY.
What…?

FIRST LADY.
THE SUN IS SHINING.
I AM TIRED,
RIDING IN AN OPEN CAR.
MY EYES ARE ITCHING
MY HAIR IS RUINED
BECAUSE OF RIDING IN AN OPEN CAR.

MY HAT WILL BE IMMORTALIZED.
I KNOW.
I KNOW.
I HAVE TO SMILE FOR PHOTOGRAPHS —
— I KNOW —
WE SMILE AND WAVE
AND DRIVE SO SLOW
PASSING HUNDREDS OF PEOPLE.
WHAT DO THEY WANT?
THOUSANDS OF VOICES.
WHAT DO THEY NEED?
ALL THAT I CAN DO IS
SMILE AND WAVE AND
SMILE AND WAVE AND
SMILE AND WAVE AND
WAVE AND WAVE AND WAVE
AND WAVE AND WAVE
AND THEN I FEEL
THE SMALLEST THING:
NOT A PAIN — BUT A PAIN.
THE SMALLEST SOUND:
NOT A VOICE — BUT A VOICE.
I FEEL THE SMALLEST THING
AS I SIT BY THE SIDE
OF MY HUSBAND.
AS A MILLION MILLION PEOPLE
BRING THE TRAFFIC TO A CRAWL
I FEEL EVERYTHING AND ALL
AND NOTHING
BUT THE SMALLEST THING ...

MARY.
    Stop this. Please stop this.
(Mary lives through the following with the First Lady; both remain in their seats, which have become, though not literally, the back seats of the Presidential limosine.)

FIRST LADY.
    THE SUN IS RUTHLESS.
    I AM SWEATING:

ROASTING IN AN OPEN CAR.
I'M SICK OF SMILING.
I'M SICK OF WAVING.
I'M SICK OF RIDING IN AN OPEN CAR.
THE DAY WILL BE IMMORTALIZED.
SO FAST.
SO FAST.
AND EVERYTHING I KNOW IS GONE —
SO FAST —
AND SUDDENLY WE'RE SPEEDING PAST
ALL THE HUNDREDS OF PEOPLE.
WHAT DO THEY SEE?
THOUSANDS OF VOICES.
WHAT DO THEY SAY?
ALL THAT I CAN DO IS
TURN AND SCREAM AND
TURN AND REACH AND
REACH AND REACH AND
REACH AND REACH AND
REACH AND REACH AND REACH
AND REACH AND FEEL
THE SMALLEST THING:
NOT A PAIN — BUT A PAIN.
THE SMALLEST SOUND:
NOT A VOICE — BUT A VOICE.
I FEEL THE SMALLEST THING:
IN THE HEAT
OF THE BLOOD
OF MY HUSBAND.
AS A MILLION MILLION FLASHBULBS
TURN THE BLOOD TO BLACK AND WHITE.
IT SINGS WITH ALL ITS MIGHT:
THE SMALLEST THING.
THE SMALLEST THING:
MY LIFE.
MY LIFE ...

(She grips Mary's arm. Mary pulls her arm free. Lady Bird Johnson re-enters.)

LADY BIRD.
    LADIES.

FIRST LADY.
    Hello again, Lady Bird.

LADY BIRD.
    Not right now, thank you ...
(She exits.)

FIRST LADY.
    LOOK, MY HAT.
    AND MY GLOVES.
    HERE IN MY HANDS.

MARY.
    IN YOUR HANDS ...

FIRST LADY.
    TIME FOR A KITTY-CAT NAP.

MARY.
    Yes ... Okay ... Sleep ...
(The First Lady curls up and falls asleep. Mary holds her, gently, tentatively.)
    Sleep ... I'm here ... Mary's here ...
(Mary nods off. The First Lady exits. Evelyn enters and sits next to Mary.)
    What?

EVELYN.
    What what?

MARY.
    DID SHE ASK FOR ME?

EVELYN.
    No. Just about there.
    DID YOU HAVE A NICE NAP?

MARY.
> Yes ...
> ... I DON'T KNOW.
> IS MRS. JOHNSON ON BOARD?

EVELYN.
> Of course not.
> THE CHIEF AND THE VICE PRESIDENT
> NEVER TRAVEL ON THE SAME PLANE.

MARY. *(Not knowing this.)*
> I knew that ... Evelyn...?

EVELYN.
> Yes?

MARY.
> I DON'T KNOW ...

EVELYN.
> NOW YOU'RE GETTING NERVOUS —
> LIKE THE REST OF US.

MARY.
> I DON'T KNOW ...

EVELYN.
> Don't worry Mary. Things'll go just fine. Where's that campaign spirit?

MARY.
> I ... I can't do anything else. Just this.

EVELYN.
> SURE YOU CAN.
> BUT THIS IS WHAT YOU DO WELL.

MARY.
> Is it...? Is it...?

EVELYN.
        Mary, Mary, Mary, Mary, Mary …
        HERE WE ARE
        JUST A SPECK IN THE AIR.
        ABOUT TO LAND
        ON A DOT DOWN THERE.
        THIS IS WHAT WE ARE:
        A SPECK.
        A DOT.
        THIS IS WHAT WE ARE.
        WE'VE CAST OUR LOT.
        WE'RE ONLY PART
        OF A GIANT MACHINE.
        WE'RE SELDOM HEARD
        AND WE'RE SELDOM SEEN.
        THIS IS WHAT WE ARE:
        THE WORK.
        THE GRIEF.
        TILL THE DAY IT ENDS,
        THERE'S NO RELIEF.
        BUT WHAT WE DO IS BOUND TO DO
        SOME GOOD.
        IT WILL, SOMEHOW.
        I BELIEVE WE'LL SEE WE DID
        SOME GOOD.
        IT'S HERE.
        RIGHT HERE.
        WE JUST CAN'T SEE IT NOW.
        NOW
        HERE WE ARE:
        LITTLE COGS IN A WHEEL
        WE'LL CHUG ALONG,
        ON THE HOPE WE FEEL.
        THE BEST IS WHAT IS ASKED OF US.
        WE'VE DONE OUR BEST SO FAR.
        SPECKS OF WORK —

MARY.
>	AND GRIEF —

EVELYN.
>	— AND HOPE

MARY.
>	THIS IS WHAT WE ARE ...

EVELYN.
>	THIS IS *ALL* WE ARE ...

MARY.
>	I MISS TOM KITTEN.

EVELYN.
>	SURE YOU DO.

MARY.
>	HE NEEDS ME.

EVELYN.
>	SURE HE DOES.

(The Aide re-enters.)

AIDE.
>	MARY GALLAGHER YOU'RE NEEDED.
>	MRS. KENNEDY WOULD LIKE YOU
>	TO BRING THE SEWING KIT.

MARY.
>	Oh, yes, indeedy! Thank you!

EVELYN.
>	Come and ride in the motorcade. It'll be fun. You deserve it.

MARY.
>	I DON'T KNOW ... Okay...! I guess...!

EVELYN.
> Look, Mary. The sun's out.
> LOOKS LIKE IT'S GOING TO BE WARM.
> I DON'T BELIEVE I'LL NEED MY COAT.

MARY.
> You're right.
> ... SHE WON'T NEED HER COAT.

(They look out the window. Mary smiles at Evelyn. Evelyn pats her hand. Mary hurries off. Evelyn continues looking out the window. Slow fade.)

THE END

PROPERTY LIST

Kit of needle and thread (MARY)
Typewriter and paper (EVELYN)
Tea tray with tea cups and tea (AIDE)

WHERE'S MAMIE?

WHERE'S MAMIE?

Ike and Mamie Eisenhower's bedroom. The White House, 1957.

King-sized bed. Pink headboard, quilted. Pink quilt, sheets, ruffles. Pink pillows with little pink flowers. Pink everything, everywhere.

Mamie is propped up in bed. She is in a pink dressing gown, pink bow in her hair, pink mules with spiked heels. It's noontime. Mamie is sulking. After a long moment of sulking.

MAMIE.
    This is the worst birthday I've ever had.... "I won't be in till late, Mamie. We'll celebrate tomorrow." Oh big-chicken-feet-deal. *Tomorrow's* not my birthday.... "There's a crisis in Little Rock, Mamie." Well pork-and-salt to you. Why doesn't he just send in the troops and shut those stupid bigots up? But no ... he has to have meetings. On my birthday.... Ha! Look at that! Footprints on the carpet! I hate that. Happy worst birthday to me.

    IN THE SHADE OF MY MOTHER'S MAGNOLIA TREE,
    YOU PROMISED YOUR LOVE UPON BENDED KNEE.
    I SAID, "I DO, I WILL, I TRUST."
    YOU SAID, "YOU MUST, YOU MUST, YOU —"

    ... "Mamie, you must not walk around with a drink in your hand even if it is just ginger ale." Yes, honey. "You know what the press will say."
    I KNOW WHAT THE PRESS WILL SAY ...
    "MRS. EISENHOWER DRINKS."
    "MRS. EISENHOWER HAS EPISODES."
    Horse baloney.
    EPISODES.
    I'LL GIVE 'EM EPISODES ...

Driver! Whadd'ya say we take her for a spin! And we won't tell Ike!

"Yes, Mrs. Eisenhower, you're the First Lady." That's right — I am!

(The Presidential limousine takes off down Pennsylvania Avenue.)

Washington, Washington! What a town! Why look at all the people! They came out just to wish me a Happy Birthday! Now that's an honor! Listen to 'em! Listen to 'em!

... "WHERE'S MAMIE?"

"WHERE'S MAMIE?"

HERE I AM!

HERE I AM!

YOU KNOW BETTER THAN THE PRESS:

WHAT YOU GET IS WHAT YOU SEE.

I CAN'T HELP ADORIN' YOU

AN' YOU CAN'T HELP ADORIN' ME!

"WHERE'S MAMIE?"

"WHERE'S MAMIE?"

OVER HERE!

HOWDY POPS!

MAMIE SMILES:

TRAFFIC STOPS!

SURE, I LIKE

BEIN' MRS. IKE

AN' I LIKE TO THINK YOU AGREE!

WHERE'S MAMIE?

HERE'S MAMIE!

SWEETHEART OF THE G.O.P.!

I'M NO OLD BESS TRUMAN

WITH A PRUNE-PIT FOR A FACE.

I'M NO ELEANOR ROOSEVELT:

I KNOW MY PLACE.

I KNOW MY JOB IS TO BE A WIFE:

MY HUSBAND'S JOB IS TO LEAD.

I GOT MY MAN WHERE I WANT HIM:

HOME!

WHAT ELSE COULD ANY GIRL NEED?

THERE'S NOTHING ELSE I NEED.

THERE'S NOTHING ELSE.

NOTHING ...

I'M NO ELEANOR ROOSEVELT ... *(An idea lights up her face.)* Stop the car! When's the next train to Little Rock? I'll go down there and see for myself about this "crisis." Maybe if I put in an appearance, those stupid bigots'll — I don't know — settle down. Which means Ike can get on home early. To his Birthday Girl. "I don't know, Mrs. E.—"
— Oh you don't know beans from a beanbag!
ALL ABOARD!

(The train takes off, bound for Little Rock.)

"WHERE'S MAMIE?"
"WHERE'S MAMIE?"
HERE SHE COMES!
HOLY SMOKES!
SHE'S NO QUEEN!
SHE'S JUST FOLKS!
I AIN'T BEEN SENT
BY THE PRESIDENT
BUT I'M BENT ON HELPING MY MAN:
WHERE'S MAMIE?
HERE'S MAMIE!
WHAT IKE CAN'T DO
MAYBE MAMIE CAN!

(Mamie arrives in Little Rock. The atmosphere seems tense, hot.)

Here I am everyone! Where is everyone? Little Rock sounds like such a happy sort of town:
"LITTLE ROCK."
But it doesn't feel happy here ...

(Marian Anderson hurries on, dressed in a beautiful, modest gown with fur wrap.)

Aah — A Negro! Don't hurt me! I know you! Marian Anderson! It's me, Miss Anderson: Mamie Eisenhower!

MARIAN.
Mrs. Eisenhower! What are you doing in Little Rock?

MAMIE.
Uh ... visiting.

MARIAN.
Friends?

MAMIE.

    Uh-huh.... *You!* It's my birthday and I thought: what better birthday treat could I have than to visit my favorite Negro opera singer!

MARIAN.

    Well! Happy Birthday! But how did you know I'd be in Little Rock?

MAMIE.

    Oh.... First Lady Intuition. Ha Ha! What *are* you doing in Little Rock?

MARIAN.

    Actually, we were just leaving. But we must hurry! We must go to Washington. We must speak to the President.

MAMIE.

    We?

MARIAN.

    The situation here is very dangerous. The Negro students who are to be integrated were turned away from Little Rock Central High this morning.

MAMIE.

    Oh, I know: it's a "crisis."

MARIAN.

    The Governor refuses to protect the children from the mob. The President must intervene! Those are such pretty pillows.

MAMIE.

    Thank you. Climb aboard, Miss Anderson.

MARIAN.

    THIS IS LITTLE ROCK, MRS. EISENHOWER.
    THERE ARE CERTAIN PLACES WHERE NEGROES,
    EVEN CELEBRITIES SUCH AS OURSELVES,
    ARE NOT WELCOMED.

MAMIE.

You'll pardon my French but that's just plain donkey balls. You're welcomed here.

(Marian smiles, accepts Mamie's invitation and climbs on board the bed.)
Grapefruit?

MARIAN.

Thank you, but no.

MAMIE.

I'll be honest: this Negro crisis has nothing to do with me. It's political. But I'm worried about Ike. His ticker isn't what it used to be.

MARIAN.

Do you understand what's happening here?

MAMIE.

Sure. Negroes want to integrate. Fine by me.

MARIAN.

But it's not fine by others. Everyone is waiting to see what the President will do. But so far, he has said nothing. He *must* take action. Today.

MAMIE.

Which would be my *birth*day. How 'bout a game? Canasta?

MARIAN.

OLD MANSION HAS TO COME DOWN —

MAMIE.

— You don't mean my White House, do you? You like my White House, don't you?

MARIAN.

Yes, but —

MAMIE.

Oh I know the D.A.R. put up a fuss about you singing in Washington that time — well between you and me, I can't stomach the D.A.R. You ever watch those women eat?

35

MARIAN.

    Yes, but —

MAMIE.

    Well, Washington is *my* town now and the White House is *my* house. Got my man where I want him: home. Sometimes.

MARIAN.

    You love your husband very much. Perhaps you could persuade him for us. After all, you are the First Lady, the closest person to the most powerful man in the world —

MAMIE.

    Now you hold on there. That's one of Ike's rules: I don't get involved. He doesn't know I'm down here in Little Rock and he'd be madder than the devil-dee-doo if he found out. I never get involved, publicly or otherwise.

MARIAN.

    But —

MAMIE.

    That's a rule.
    ... MY HUSBAND WAS AN ARMY MAN.
    WE LIVED WHERE HE WAS STATIONED.
    IN PANAMA — WITH BUGS AS BIG AS AIRPLANES.
    THE PHILIPPINES — WITH RATS THE SIZE OF TANKS.
    I STUCK IT OUT.
    MADE HIM A HOME.
    MANAGED THE BOOKS.
    PINCHED EVERY CENT.
    GAVE HIM A SON.
    GAVE HIM A SON ...
    AND I WOULDN'T CHANGE A SINGLE THING.
    NOT THE BARRACKS WITH THE BAD LATRINES.
    NOT THE CHATTER OF THE ARMY WIVES.

I DID NOT COMPLAIN.
MY HUSBAND WAS AN ARMY MAN.
I HAD RULES TO FOLLOW.

MY HUSBAND WAS A GENERAL.
HE WON THE WAR IN EUROPE.
IN NORMANDY — WITH BOMBS AS BIG AS BUILDINGS.
IN GERMANY — WITH RATS THE SIZE OF MEN.
I STUCK IT OUT.
WAITED AT HOME.
GOT GOOD AT BRIDGE.
WAITED FOR MONTHS.
WAITED FOR YEARS.
WAITED ALONE ...

BUT I WOULDN'T CHANGE A SINGLE THING.
NOT THE WAITING FOR THE WAR TO END.
NOT THE WAITING FOR A NORMAL LIFE.
WHAT'S A NORMAL LIFE?
MY HUSBAND WAS A GENERAL.
I HAD RULES TO FOLLOW.

AND BOY-OH-BOY I KNEW IT WAY BACK WHEN:
MY HANDSOME GUY WAS NOT LIKE OTHER MEN.
MY HANDSOME GUY WAS MINE ALL RIGHT,
BUT THEN:
THE ARMY CAME FIRST, THE WAR CAME FIRST,
THE COUNTRY CAME FIRST, THE PEOPLE CAME FIRST,
EVERYTHING AND EVERYBODY ELSE CAME FIRST
AND NOW —

MY HUSBAND IS THE PRESIDENT.
AND WE LIVE IN THE WHITE HOUSE.
IN WASHINGTON — WITH MOUTHS AS BIG AS POTHOLES
IN WASHINGTON — WITH MEN THE SIZE OF RATS.
I'VE STUCK IT OUT:
MADE HIM A HOME.
SHOOK LOTS OF HANDS.
DEALT WITH THE PRESS.

>RUMORS AND LIES.
>RUMORS AND LES ...
>AND I WOULDN'T CHANGE A SINGLE THING.
>EVERYTHING I WANTED, I GOT.
>SURE, I MIGHT'VE MISSED SOME THINGS;
>I WILL NOT COMPLAIN.
>MY HUSBAND IS AN ARMY MAN.
>GENERAL.
>PRESIDENT.
>I HAVE RULES TO FOLLOW ...

MARIAN.
>OLD RULES ARE OLD RULES.
>NEW RULES ARE BETTER.

MAMIE.
>What?

MARIAN.
>YOU HAVEN'T HEARD THE MOB.
>YOU HAVEN'T SEEN THEIR FACES, MRS. E.
>May we call you that?
>"MRS. E."?

MAMIE.
>Sure.

MARIAN.
>AND WHILE THE PRESIDENT WAITS, THE MOB GROWS.
>WHILE THE PRESIDENT WAITS, THE MOB RULES.
>WHILE THE PRESIDENT WAITS AND WAITS
>THE HATE BLOSSOMS.
>"GO HOME, NIGGER!"
>"KNOW YOUR PLACE, NIGGER!"
>"KILL THE NIGGER CHILDREN!"
>"KILL THE NIGGER CHILDREN ..."

MAMIE.
> CHILDREN ...

MARIAN.
> WHILE THE PRESIDENT WAITS, SO DO CHILDREN.
> WHO WILL TEACH THEM?
> WHO WILL SPEAK FOR THEM?
> WHO WILL MAKE THE NEW RULES?
> WHO WILL BREAK THE OLD RULES?
>
> MELBA!
> GLORIA!
> MINNIE JEAN!
> COME TO SCHOOL, CHILDREN.
> WE ARE ALL LEARNING
> AS THE WORLD'S TURNING
> THAT THE CHANGE MUST COME TONIGHT.
> THERE'S A DRUM BEATING
> WHERE THE SUN'S MEETING
> WITH THE STARS
> AND ALL THE STARS THEY KNOW
> THE CHANGE
> MUST COME TONIGHT.
> OLD MANSION HAS TO COME DOWN.
> NEW MANSION HAS TO GO UP.
> NEW MANSION HAS TO RISE HIGH.
> AND ALL THAT'S OLD GET READY TO DIE.
> GET READY, GET READY, GET READY, GET READY —
>
> MELBA!
> GLORIA!
> MINNIE JEAN!
> COME TO SCHOOL, CHILDREN.
> THERE'S A NEW TEACHING
> AND THE OLD TEACHING
> HAS TO GET THE BOOT TONIGHT.
> THERE'S A DRUM POUNDING
> AND THE SKY'S ROUNDING UP
> THE STARS

AND ALL THE STARS CAN'T STOP
THE CHANGE
THAT'S COMING TONIGHT...!

MAMIE.

I know what it feels like; not being allowed in. Ike won't let me near the Oval Office. But we gotta do something, don't we?

MARIAN.

Yes!

MAMIE.

We gotta stand up to Ike and tell him what we think, don't we?

MARIAN.

Then you'll speak to your husband?

MAMIE.

Well. No. But maybe I can arrange for *you* to see him. Right now.

MARIAN.

Could you?

MAMIE.

Sure! Come on! All ashore that's going ashore!

MARIAN.

But —

MAMIE.

First-class passengers to the left! Second-class passengers to the right! Steerage — down! (You stick with me, Miss Anderson. No one will give you any trouble as long as you're with me.)

MARIAN.

We thought we were going to see the President!

MAMIE.

> We are!

MARION.

> On a boat?

MAMIE.

> Oh Captain, this Negro woman is my friend and a celebrity and she's traveling with me! "Most certainly, Mrs. Eisenhower." To Algiers!

MARIAN.

> Algiers?

(The boat sets sail across the Atlantic.)

MAMIE.

> Ike was stationed there in '44. Commander-in-Chief of the Allied Forces. We're going back in time to pay him a surprise!

MARIAN.

> We don't want to go back in time!

MAMIE.

> We want to see about some rumors and lies.

MARIAN.

> What rumors? What lies?!

MAMIE.

> You want to change some things, don't you? Well so do I!

MARIAN.

> CHANGE IS FOR THE PRESENT, MRS. E;
> NOT FOR THE PAST —

MAMIE.

> You want to see the President, don't you?

MARIAN.

    Yes —

MAMIE.

    Well you're gonna see the future President!
(The Atlantic turns threatening. German submarines prowl the waters. Distant explosions.)

MARIAN.

    This is dangerous!

MAMIE.

    I know.... Come on, remember that song?
    IN ALGIERS ...

MARIAN.

    IN ALGIERS ...

(Mamie and Marian sing together; this being an old favorite of Mamie's, such as "Bali Ha'i" from South Pacific, *perhaps the number is embellished with choreography à la "Happy Talk.")*

MAMIE/MARIAN.

    IN ALGIERS
    I'LL FIND YOU,
    WHERE THE SUN BURNS THE SAND.
    IN ALGIERS
    I'LL REMIND YOU
    HOW FAR AWAY YOU ARE
    IN A FARAWAY LAND.
    IN ALGIERS
    I'LL CALL YOU
    FROM A TALL MINARET.
    WILL YOU COME
    WHEN I CALL YOU?
    OR WILL YOU TURN AWAY
    NEVER FEELING REGRET?
    WILL YOU TURN AWAY?
    WILL YOU TURN AWAY?
    WILL YOU TURN AWAY?
    OUR DREAMS ARE MIRAGES

>   SET ON A DESERT HILL.
>   WE'LL STRUGGLE TO REACH THEM;
>   WE'LL TRY— BUT WE NEVER WILL ...

(Algiers appears on the horizon. Ike and his Chauffeur dance on. Mamie recognizes Ike.)

MARIAN.
>   BY AND BY,
>   I'LL LOSE YOU,
>   WHERE THE WIND
>   STIRS THE SAND
>   AND I'LL CRY:
>   'WHERE ARE YOU LOVER?'
>   'WHERE ARE YOU LOVER?'

MAMIE.
>   WHERE ARE YOU LOVER?

MARIAN.
>   MY CRY OF LOVE THAT'S LOST
>   WILL NEVER REACH YOUR EARS.
>   THE SUN WILL BURN OUR HEARTS
>   IN ALGIERS ...

MAMIE.
>   I think we've arrived.

MARIAN.
>   Why did you bring us here!

MAMIE.
>   Shhh ...

MARIAN.
>   Isn't that President Eisenhower?

MAMIE.
>   General Eisenhower. I forgot he'd look younger ...

IKE.
>BY AND BY,
>I'LL LOSE YOU,
>WHERE THE WIND
>STIRS THE SAND;
>AND I'LL CRY:
>'WHERE ARE YOU LOVER?'
>'WHERE ARE YOU LOVER?'

MAMIE.
>Where are you, lover...?

IKE. *(To his Chauffeur.)*
>Let's go back to headquarters. You get the jeep.

(The Chauffeur kisses Ike.)

MAMIE.
>RUMORS AND LES.
>RUMORS AND LIES ...
>That's his chauffeur.

MARIAN.
>Is this why you dragged us here! To spy on your husband!

MAMIE.
>Yes!

MARIAN.
>We wanted to speak to the President! You told us —

MAMIE.
>I told you I could arrange for you to *see* him.

MARIAN.
>Trick! Trick!

MAMIE.
>Shhh! I've got a plan.

(Mamie whispers in Marian's ear.)

MARIAN.
>We will not be involved in any scandal.
>... WE ARE A PROFESSIONAL.

MAMIE.
>Well I guess *we'll* just have to go back to Little Rock and *we'll* never get to speak to Ike, will *we?*

MARIAN.
>Very well.

IKE. *(Saluting his Chauffeur.)*
>I have to use the john.

(He exits briefly. The Chauffeur gets into her jeep. Mamie pops up beside her.)

MAMIE.
>Excuse me. That's a pretty scarf. May I see it?

CHAUFFEUR.
>Who —?

MAMIE.
>I adore this scarf. So feminine...!

(Mamie grabs the Chauffeur. She stuffs one of her pink fluffy mules into the Chauffeur's mouth. Marian holds her down.)

>I got you! Hold on tight, Miss Anderson!

MARIAN.
>We're trying —

(Mamie ties the Chauffeur up.)

MAMIE.
>Little Miss Pretty Irish Girl. It said so in the photograph in Life. The General's Chauffeur. Ha. Ha. Wanna know who I am?

THE GENERAL'S WIFE!
I KNOW YOU WORKING GIRL TYPES.
YOU TAKE ADVANTAGE OF A MAN
BEING AWAY FROM HIS WIFE.
YOU THROW YOURSELF AT MARRIED MEN
AND CALL IT A CAREER. HA!

MARIAN.

Your husband's coming!

MAMIE.

Stuff her in the back seat — Get down and keep her quiet. I'll drive.

MARIAN.

You'll kill us all!
(Mamie disguises herself as the Chauffeur.)

IKE.

Let's go ...

MAMIE.

"Yes, sir, General."
(Mamie starts up the jeep. She doesn't know how to drive.)

IKE.

REMIND ME THAT I HAVE TO WIRE MAMIE —
(The jeep lurches.)
    — Watch it!
    ... IT'S HER BIRTHDAY TODAY—
(Mamie hits a deep pothole.)
    — Keep your eyes on the road for godsakes!

MAMIE.

"All that dancing made me dizzy, Sir."

IKE.

WHAT PRESENTS SHOULD I GET FOR MAMIE?

MAMIE.
>PRESENTS?!

IKE.
>Watch it —!

(The jeep crashes. Marian screams.)
>What's wrong with you? What's going on?

(He tears off Mamie's disguise.)
>Mamie!

(The Chauffeur squeals beneath Marian.)
>What is this foolishness! Mamie! What are you doing here!

MAMIE.
>Well ... Miss Anderson here, wanted to speak to you. Miss Anderson, what was it you wanted to say?

MARIAN.
>I ... I ...

IKE.
>Who are you?

MAMIE.
>This is Marian Anderson, Ike. The opera singer.

IKE.
>Well ... what?

MARIAN. *(This is her big moment. Calmly, dignified, she stands up to the future President.)*
>Someday, sir, in Little Rock, Arkansas there'll be a crisis ... Negro students who are to be integrated will be turned away by an angry white mob ... these children will look to you, the President, for protection. Send in the troops, Sir.

IKE.
>President? Me?

MARIAN. *(Crumbling.)*
— Oh this is ridiculous!

IKE.
— Little Rock? What's going on here?

MARIAN. *(At Mamie.)*
Don't you realize the seriousness of what's happening in your country?

IKE.
Mamie! You know better than to interfere! You know the rules!

MAMIE.
OLD RULES ARE OLD RULES
BUT NEW RULES ARE BETTER ...

IKE.
What?

MAMIE.
I SAID I WOULDN'T CHANGE A SINGLE THING.
BUT I WOULD.
I WOULD CHANGE WHAT HAPPENED HERE.
WITH YOU AND HER.
AND ALL THE RUMORS EVER AFTER.
I STUCK IT OUT.
MADE YOU A HOME — WHEREVER WAS HOME.
GAVE YOU A SON.
GAVE YOU A SON.
I FOLLOWED ALL THE RULES.
EVERY SINGLE, STUPID, PIGEON-SHIT RULE.

IKE.
Mamie!

MAMIE.
BOY-OH-BOY, I KNEW IT WAY BACK WHEN,
MY HANDSOME GUY WAS NOT LIKE OTHER MEN:
MY HANDSOME GUY WAS MINE ALL RIGHT

BUT THEN:
THE ARMY CAME FIRST, THE WAR CAME FIRST.
AND *SHE* CAME FIRST —

IKE.

You go home, Mamie —

MAMIE.

"GO HOME, MAMIE."
"KNOW YOUR PLACE, MAMIE."
MAMIE SHOULDN'T THINK.
MAMIE SHOULDN'T SPEAK.
MAMIE'S NOT ALLOWED.
WHAT'S MAMIE?
WHO'S MAMIE?

IKE.

Now you stop that ...

MAMIE.

Well ... now I know the truth. What do I do with it?
(Ike doesn't know what to do. Marian nudges him to comfort his wife.)

IKE.

SOMEDAY WE'LL OWN A HOUSE.
AND WE WILL CALL IT HOME.
YOU'LL PAINT IT ALL IN PINK.
I'LL PLANT AND MOW THE LAWN.
AND WE'LL WONDER WHERE THE TIME HAS GONE.
TOMORROW I WILL LOVE YOU MORE.
HONEST.
MAMIE.
TOMORROW I WILL LOVE YOU MORE.

MARIAN.

WHAT IS PAST IS PAST.
WHAT IS THEN IS THEN.
HOW TO CHANGE THE PAST
ELUDES THE SMARTEST MEN.

        NOTHING YOU CAN DO
        CAN EVER CHANGE WHAT WAS.
        SO WHY NOT LOOK AHEAD
        LIKE EVERY LOVER DOES.
(Mamie joins Ike and Marian.)

MAMIE/IKE/MARIAN.
    SOMEDAY WE'LL OWN A HOUSE.
    AND WE WILL CALL IT HOME.

MAMIE/MARIAN.
    I'LL TELL YOU WHAT I THINK.

IKE.
    I'LL SHARE YOUR BED AT NIGHT.

MAMIE/IKE.
    AND I'LL HOLD YOU IN MY ARMS TILL DAWN.
    FOREVER I WILL LOVE YOU MORE.

MAMIE.
    BIRTHDAYS.

IKE.
    PEACETIME.

MARIAN. *(To Ike.)*
    CHILDREN.

IKE. *(To Marian.)*
    PROMISE.

MAMIE.
    HUSBAND.

CHAUFFEUR.
    (Help me)

IKE/MAMIE.
>TOMORROW I WILL LOVE YOU MORE.

(Ike and Mamie embrace.)

IKE.
> Well girls, if you'll excuse me, I've got a war to wrap up. There's a B-29 all set to fly you back stateside.

MAMIE.
> Come on, Miss Anderson, we've got work to do in Washington.

IKE.
> Happy Birthday, Birthday Girl.

(He kisses the top of her head and retrieves his Chauffeur. They exit.)

MAMIE.
> I hate flying. "Fasten your seatbelt, Miss Anderson." Off we go!! Hurry us home boys! We got work to do! We're gonna send in the troops! Hey, this isn't so bad after all! Look at the Atlantic!

MARIAN.
> BLUER THAN BLUE ...

MAMIE.
> This is the best birthday ever! We can see the world from here! We can see everything!

THE END

SOUND EFFECTS

Distant explosions

OLIO

OLIO

Sign: "WELCOME! CHRISTIAN DEMOCRAT MOTHERS AND DAUGH-TERS!"

Bess and her daughter Margaret enter. Margaret is in a pretty gown. Bess carries a purse.

BESS.

This is my daughter Margaret Truman. She would like to sing for you.... I'm not doing a thing.... And if you don't like her singing you can just not.

MARGARET.

Mommy.

BESS.

Well? Go on. No one's stopping you. You wanted to do the singing.

MARGARET.

Mommy, please. *(To the audience.)* This is a song I chose in honor of my father and my mother.

BESS.

Why, thank you. Well ... go on. I'm not doing nothing.
(Music begins. As Margaret sings, Bess develops a cough. She searches through her purse for a candy. She finds one, wrapped in noisy wax paper. She sucks on the candy. She crunches it. She has to blow her nose, too.)

MARGARET.

WON'T YOU LAY ME TO REST
IN OLE MISSOURA
WHERE THE RIVER RUNS BUT
TIME STANDS STILLY-STILL.
LET ME FIND LASTING PEACE

>IN OLE MISSOURA
>WITH THE ONE I LOVE WHO LOVES ME
>AND SWEARS HE ALWAYS WILL.
>THE TROUBLES OF THE WORLD
>WILL TROUBLE ME NO MORE;
>NO POLITICS, NO WASHINGTON
>AND NO ATOMIC WAR.
>IF I NEVER RETURN
>TO OLE MISSOURA
>THEN A RESTLESS SPIRIT
>EVER SHALL I ROAM;
>WON'T YOU LAY ME,
>WON'T YOU LAY ME,
>LAY ME! LAY ME! LAY ME!
>WON'T YOU LAY ME TO REST
>IN OLE MISSOURA
>MY NEVER-CHANGING, TIME-FORGOTTEN,
>HOME-FOREVER-HOME ...

BESS.
>That it?

MARGARET.
>Oh Mommy ...
(She runs off in tears.)

BESS.
>Very nice. My daughter, Margaret. The singer.

THE END

PROPERTY LIST

Purse (BESS) with:
    hard candy in paper wrapper
    tissues

ELEANOR SLEEPS HERE

ELEANOR SLEEPS HERE

The cockpit and backspace of Amelia Earhart's Lockheed Electra. 1935. Night. The tiny aeroplane flies. Amelia pilots. Eleanor sits next to her. They face upstage. In the backspace of the plane, by the fuel tanks, Hick squats, facing the audience. All the women are in formal evening attire, Amelia with leather aviator cap.

ELEANOR.
>This is the beginning of a new era
>in human flight!
>WE SHALL DEMONSTRATE THAT IT IS SAFE TO FLY
>FROM WASHINGTON TO BALTIMORE AND BACK
>IN THE MIDDLE OF THE NIGHT
>AND LAND, SAFELY.
>FRANKLIN WILL BE JEALOUS.
>BUT I'M GLAD THAT I MENTIONED OVER DINNER
>THAT I'VE NEVER EVER FLOWN.
>I LOVE A WHIM!
>THANK YOU, AMELIA.
>What do you say, Hick?

HICK. *(Not fine.)*
>FINE.

ELEANOR.
>You were awfully quiet at dinner.
>SHE DOESN'T LIKE HENRIETTA NESBITT'S COOKING.
>WHO'S GOT A LIFESAVER?
>HICK...?

HICK.
>I think I have ... a roll ... in my.... Here.

ELEANOR.
>YUM YUM.

HICK. *(Over-polite.)*
    Miss Earhart?

AMELIA.
    It's your last one.

ELEANOR.
    Oh, take it, Amelia.
    HICK'S GOT A PURSE FULL OF TOOTSIE ROLLS.

AMELIA. *(Taking Hick's last Lifesaver.)*
    Thank you.... Having fun, Miss Hickok?

ELEANOR. *(Before Hick can answer.)*
    Hick's a sport.
    SHE'S GONE DOWN INTO COALMINES WITH ME,
    UP INTO MOUNTAINS WITH ME.
    I bet she'd love to join you on your trip around the world! Wouldn't that make a good column for "My Day," Hick! Our flight over the Pacific Ocean!

HICK. *(To herself.)*
    HEADLINE:
    "FIRST LADY OF UNITED STATES
    AND FIRST LADY OF FLIGHT
    HOP ON A PLANE ON AN AFTER-DINNER WHIM
    CRASH INTO CAPITOL BUILDING.
    CONGRESS SLAUGHTERED."

AMELIA.
    What is it you do at the White House, Miss Hickok?

HICK. *(To herself.)*
    OTHER CASUALTIES.

ELEANOR.
    Hick's living there for the time being — she does field reporting for the Federal Emergency Relief project — AND SHE HELPS ME. What's that dial for?

HICK. *(To herself.)*
OH MISS EARHART WITH YOUR OWN FASHION LINE.
AND THE TOOTHPASTE.
AND THE GUM.
Eleanor's got secretaries. Eleanor's got maids. Eleanor's got plenty of friends and plenty of help. What's it I do? Good question ...

I LIVE IN THE WHITE HOUSE.
I SLEEP ON A COT.
IN A DUSTY LITTLE HALLWAY
NEXT TO ELEANOR'S ROOM.
I DON'T MIND THE WHITE HOUSE.
I AVOID THE FOOD.
I'VE GOTTEN USED TO LIVING
OUTSIDE ELEANOR'S ROOM.
WANNA KNOW
WHY WOULD A TOP-NOTCH WORLD-CLASS
ONE-OF-THE-BOYS FEMALE JOURNALIST
GIVE EVERYTHING UP
TO RUN AFTER, CHASE AFTER,
CARRY, TOTE AND STUMBLE AFTER
TRAIL AFTER ELEANOR ROOSEVELT
LIKE A PRESIDENTIAL PUP?
Why? Don't ask ...

I COULD WRITE ABOUT THE WHITE HOUSE.
HICK HAS GOT THE SCOOP.
I KNOW WHO'S BEEN DOING WHAT TO WHOM.
A GOOD REPORTER HAS TO HAVE PERSPECTIVE;
SHE CAN'T BE OVER-ZEALOUS OR SELECTIVE;
AND MOST OF ALL, SHE HAS TO STAY OBJECTIVE.
WHO CAN STAY OBJECTIVE
LIVING IN THE WHITE HOUSE
SLEEPING ON A COT.
IN A DUSTY LITTLE HALLWAY
OUTSIDE
CLOSE TO

TOO CLOSE TO
ELEANOR'S ROOM?

ELEANOR.
    Tell Amelia your monkey fur story, Hick.

HICK. *(To Eleanor.)*
    No.

ELEANOR.
    — When she was with the A.P., she had an interview with a famous opera singer and Hick wore a new suit with a monkey fur collar.

HICK.
    Eleanor ...

ELEANOR.
    ... And it began to rain and Hick got soaked. Then this opera singer —

HICK. *(To herself.)*
    — GERALDINE FARRAR. HORRIBLE WOMAN.

ELEANOR.
    — kept her waiting and Hick smelled this odor. Hick's wet monkey fur began to stink! Ha!

HICK.
    Ha.

AMELIA.
    When I first flew the Atlantic I experienced a similar embarrassing odor.

ELEANOR.
    Oh my ... what was it?

AMELIA.
    I don't know.

HICK. *(To herself.)*
>WET AVIATRIX.
>Ha!

ELEANOR.
>What Hick?

HICK. *(To Eleanor.)*
>NOTHING.

(To herself.)
>"When I first flew the Atlantic ..."
>OH MISS EARHART.
>YOU DIDN'T "FLY" THE ATLANTIC.
>A MAN DID.
>YOU WENT ALONG FOR THE RIDE.
>THE REST YOUR HUSBAND MADE UP.
>He invented you.
>I INVENTED ELEANOR.
>No one invented me.
>JUST REMEMBER THAT.

ELEANOR.
>WHO'S GOT A TOOTSIE ROLL? HICK?

HICK.
>Here ...

(Overly friendly.)
>MISS EARHART?

AMELIA.
>No thank you.

HICK. *(Not friendly, to herself.)*
>"NO THANK YOU"
>"NO THANK YOU"
>YOU ARE SO POLITE.
>YOU ARE A VERY NICE AVIATRIX.
>WITH A TERRIBLE HAIRCUT.

Oh, I've seen your fashion line. "Functional Clothes for the Functioning Woman." Your husband sure comes up with some wild schemes to peddle your fanny, doesn't he? *(To Amelia.)* May I smoke, Miss Earhart?

ELEANOR.

Lorena! Put that cigar away.

AMELIA.

It's best you refrain. You're close to the gas tank.

HICK.

Of course ...
(To herself.)
OF COURSE I'M CLOSE TO THE GAS TANK.
HEADLINE:
"FIRST LADY OF UNITED STATES
AND FIRST LADY OF FLIGHT
EXPLODE IN THE AIR
WHEN EX-REPORTER LIGHTS CIGAR.
PLANE CRASHES IN THE ATLANTIC.
FISH KILLED."

ELEANOR.

You wouldn't, would you, Hick?

HICK. *(To Eleanor.)*
Wouldn't what?

ELEANOR.

Tell Franklin if I took over the controls
... AND FLEW THE PLANE MYSELF?

HICK. *(To herself.)*
WHO TAUGHT YOU TO SAY WHAT YOU WANT
AND TO SAY HOW YOU'LL GET IT?
WHAT WHERE WHEN WHY
WHO?

ELEANOR.
> Hick?

HICK. *(To Eleanor.)*
> Yes I'd tell Franklin.

ELEANOR.
> We are cranky tonight.

HICK.
> Yes we are.

ELEANOR.
> Yes we are.

AMELIA.
> My husband says it would be a publicity coup if Eleanor flew.

ELEANOR.
> SEE? YOU'D HAVE A SCOOP, HICK.

HICK. *(To herself.)*
> I don't scoop anymore. Remember? Inauguration Eve? You read me Franklin's speech? "We have nothing to fear but fear itself."
> BIGGEST SCOOP OF MY LIFE.
> BIGGEST SCOOP OF ANYONE'S LIFE.
> DID I BREAK IT TO THE WIRE?
> NO.
> AND I KNEW I WAS DONE FOR.
> RIGHT THEN AND THERE, OH YES ...
> "WE HAVE NOTHING TO FEAR BUT FEAR ..."
> OH YES ...

ELEANOR. *(In the middle of a conversation with Amelia.)*
> ... Of course, I'll do that. I'll tell Franklin to appoint someone who supports the training of women pilots — I do truly love your gown.

AMELIA.
>Thank you. I designed it myself.

ELEANOR.
>What a talent you are!

HICK. *(To herself.)*
>I NEED A SMOKE.

(She stands up, breaking the boundaries of the plane. She steps carefully out onto the wing.)

>God. Must be Washington. That dingy little glow....
>AND LOOK AT YOU THERE
>TWO FAMOUS WOMEN
>UP IN THE AIR.
>TWO FAMOUS WOMEN
>WITH UNRULY HAIR.
>HEROES FOR THE DEPRESSION.

(She lights up her cigar.)

>Ah.... That's good.
>NOTHING LIKE A SMOKE WHILE
>STANDING ON THE WING
>OF A DANGEROUS AIRCRAFT
>FLYING THROUGH THE NIGHT.
>HEADLINE:
>"EX-REPORTER LEAPS FROM SPEEDING
>CHICKEN COOP—
>>'SHE WANTED TO FLY'
>WITNESSES SAY ..."

(Hick enjoys the night air and dances a bit on the wing ... gingerly at first, then happily.)

ELEANOR. *(Addressing Hick, as though Hick were still in the back of the plane.)*
>Couldn't I, Hick?

HICK. *(From the wing, to Eleanor.)*
>What?

ELEANOR.
>Find time for lessons.

HICK.
> Lessons?

ELEANOR.
> Flying lessons with Amelia.

HICK.
> The nation needs Mrs. Roosevelt in one piece.

ELEANOR.
> Oh Lorena.

(Hick stops dancing.)

HICK. *(To herself.)*
> "OH LORENA."
> LIKE IT'S COSTING HER MONEY
> SAYING MY NAME.
> "OH LORENA."
> THAT NEVER HAPPENED
> BEFORE SHE BECAME
> MRS. ROOSEVELT.
> "MY DAY"
> "FRANKLIN'S LEGS"
> VISIONARY.
> TEACHER.
> SINCE WHEN DID ELEANOR BECOME
> THE TEACHER?
>
> OH, MISS EARHART WITH THE FAMOUS FACE ...
> WANNA HEAR A REALLY FUNNY STORY?
> HERE'S THE FUNNY STORY OF THE FIRST LADY'S PAL.
> NOW, HOW DOES ONE BECOME THE FIRST LADY'S PAL?
> DON'T ASK — ALL RIGHT — I'LL TELL YOU:
>
> Chapter One.
>
> DIRT POOR GIRL FROM THE DULL MIDWEST
> NEARLY RISES TO THE TOP

OF WHAT EVER IS THE TOP
OF A MOUNTAIN RULED BY MEN.
SHE'S 'ALMOST SOMEONE FAMOUS' —
'ALMOST SOMEONE GREAT' BUT THEN:

ON ONE FATAL DAY
ON A SLOW MOVING TRAIN
THIS 'ALMOST SOMEONE FAMOUS' MEETS
ELEANOR.
IN ONE FATAL HOUR
AND WITHOUT ANY PAIN.
THIS "ALMOST SOMEONE GREAT' FALLS.
SHE KNOWS HER DAYS ARE NUMBERED
IN HALF.
WHEN SHE HEARS ELEANOR'S LAUGH.
WHEN SHE SEES ELEANOR'S SMILE.
WHEN SHE WRITES DOWN ELEANOR'S WORDS.
WHEN SHE SHAKES ELEANOR'S HAND.
ELEANOR'S HAND, ELEANOR'S HAND ...

Chapter Two.

HOTSHOT PRIZE OF THE A.P. WIRE
BECOMES THE NEW FIRST LADY'S PAL.
NOT A PRESS GAL PAL, *THE* PAL
IN A CITY RULED BY MEN
SHE'S "IN" BUT ON HER GUARD TO STAY
OBJECTIVE, OH BUT THEN
ON ONE FATAL DAY
HER DEFENSES DROOP
AND THIS 'ALMOST SOMEONE FAMOUS' LOVES
ELEANOR.
SHE PUTS DOWN HER PEN
WHEN SHE SHOULD GET THE SCOOP
AND THIS 'ALMOST SOMEONE GREAT'
DIES.
IN CHAPTERS THREE TO TEN
SHE DIES AND DIES AGAIN
WHEN SHE HEARS ELEANOR'S LAUGH.

WHEN SHE SEES ELEANOR'S SMILE.
WHEN SHE WATCHES ELEANOR RISE.
WHEN SHE HOLDS ELEANOR'S HAND.
ELEANOR'S HAND, ELEANOR'S HAND ...

ELEANOR. *(In the middle of a conversation with Amelia.)*
If the D.A.R. want to support rearmament, they should be willing to support the right of women to bear arms in combat as well.

AMELIA. *(Reciting, to Eleanor.)*
'Oh! Yes! I agree with you!'

HICK. *(To herself.)*
You agree with *me*. Before she met me Eleanor thought grappling with an issue meant trying to get through a copy of *Harper's Bazaar*.

GREATNESS ISN'T BORN.
GREATNESS IS INSPIRED
AND ONCE IT'S BEEN ABSORBED,
THE SOURCE IS RETIRED.
LIKE A WHINY OLD DOG.
Say, "Thank you, Hick."
SAY "THANK YOU, HICK, FOR CREATING ME."

AMELIA. *(Reciting, to Eleanor.)*
Freedom, solitude, both I own.
Alone, alive, I float;
Breathless as the racing stars.

ELEANOR.
What's that?

AMELIA.
It's a poem I wrote.

ELEANOR.
Amelia's a poetess as well. *(Eleanor turns around to smile at Hick in the back seat. It's the first time we've seen Eleanor full face.)* Isn't that remarkable, Hick?

HICK. *(Still out on the wing.)*
    Yes, it's remarkable ...
(Eleanor's face is frozen in time, her smile contains a multitude of feelings.)
    WHEN ELEANOR SMILES AT ME
    WHEN ELEANOR SMILES IT HURTS HER.
    SHE'S TRYING TO HIDE
    WHAT'S FINISHED INSIDE
    WHEN ELEANOR SMILES AT ME,
    WHEN ELEANOR SMILES AT ME.
(Lights fade on Eleanor's face and on the plane. Hick remains isolated on the wing.)

    WHEN ELEANOR LOOKS AT ME,
    WHAT ELEANOR SEES DISTURBS HER.
    SHE TRIES TO HANG ON
    WHILE WISHING ME GONE
    WHEN ELEANOR LOOKS AT ME,
    WHEN ELEANOR LOOKS AT ME.

    SHE WANTS TOMORROW.
    I AM PAST.
    I STOPPED GROWING LONG AGO.
    ELEANOR GREW TOO FAST.

    WHAT DID ELEANOR TAKE FROM ME?
    WHAT ELEANOR TOOK WAS GREATNESS.
    I KNEW WHAT WOULD BE
    LONG BEFORE SHE.
    WHAT ELEANOR TOOK FROM ME
    I LET ELEANOR TAKE FROM ME ...

    OH, MISS EARHART WITH THE PICTURE
    IN THE PAPER EVERY DAY;
    DON'T GET TOO CLOSE TO MY FRIEND.
    SHE'LL SWALLOW YOU.
    AND DROWN YOU
    AND WORST OF ALL,
    SHE'LL WRITE YOU LETTERS ...

ELEANOR.   *(Eleanor now appears facing front. She seems to float in the night sky as the two women sing.)*
"DEAREST HICK, YOU ARE A GENIUS.
I RELY ON YOU AS ALWAYS ..."

HICK.   *(Facing front.)*
— And you'll keep them in a box underneath your bed.

ELEANOR.
"DEAREST HICK, I HAVE TAKEN YOUR ADVICE."

HICK.
— And you'll hate yourself for keeping them.

ELEANOR.
"YOUR WISDOM ALWAYS LEADS ME TO CONCLUSIONS
I NEVER WOULD HAVE REACHED ON MY OWN."

HICK.
— And you'll hate what you've become.

ELEANOR.
"YOU HAVE GROWN TO BE A PART OF ME.
I CANNOT GO THIS WAY ALONE."

HICK.
— And you'll burn the most personal ones.

ELEANOR.
"THE SMILE ON YOUR FACE AS GERSHWIN PLAYED
LAST NIGHT ..."

HICK.
I remember.

ELEANOR.
"THE SOFTNESS OF YOUR HAND IN MINE ..."

HICK.
>   — AS WE SAT IN THE GARDEN

ELEANOR.
>   "IN THE CEMETERY ..."

HICK.
>   — THAT JANUARY MORNING

ELEANOR.
>   "THE STATUE ..."

HICK.
>   — OF THE WOMAN IN SORROW.

ELEANOR/HICK.
>   "OUR STATUE CALLED GRIEF."

(The women begin to turn slowly, eventually facing each other.)

ELEANOR.
>   "THE TONES IN YOUR VOICE."

HICK.
>   — THE TOUCH OF YOUR HAIR.

ELEANOR.
>   "THE NORTHWEST CORNER ..."

HICK.
>   — OF YOUR UPPER LIP.

ELEANOR.
>   "I CAN'T LET GO."

HICK.
>   — I CAN'T LET GO.

ELEANOR.
"I'LL BE SAYING OVER THOUGHT WAVES."

HICK.
— OVER THOUGHT WAVES ...

ELEANOR/HICK.
"GOODNIGHT MY FRIEND.
ANGELS WATCH OVER THEE.
GOD WATCH OVER THEE.
MY LOVE ENFOLD THEE
ALL THE NIGHT THROUGH."

(Eleanor disappears. Hick is left alone on the wing. After a slight pause, Eleanor is discovered as she was, sitting next to Amelia.)

ELEANOR.
I want to get an aviator's license. What do you say, Hick?

HICK. *(To herself.)*
WHO TAUGHT YOU TO SAY WHAT YOU WANT
AND TO SAY HOW YOU'LL GET IT?
WHAT WHERE WHEN WHY
WHO?

STOP PRETENDING YOU'RE WAITING
FOR MY ANSWER.
YOU'RE MRS. ROOSEVELT, NOW.
LET GO.

ELEANOR.
Hick?

HICK. *(To Eleanor; coldly, tightly.)*
No. Learning to fly would be impractical for you.

ELEANOR.
But.... *(Sadly.)* Yes. It would be impractical.

HICK. *(To herself.)*
>OH MISS EARHART, ELEANOR'S NEW FRIEND …
>
>DO YOU KNOW WHERE ELEANOR SLEEPS?
>WHEN AND IF SHE EVER SLEEPS?
>ELEANOR SLEEPS HERE.
>
>AND I TRY TO PUSH HER AWAY.
>I TRY AND DON'T SUCCEED.
>WHICH ONLY MAKES FOR PAIN
>THE TWO OF US DON'T NEED.
>DO YOU KNOW THAT ELEANOR'S SCARED?
>SHE WON'T LET YOU SEE HER FEAR.
>BUT AFTER ELEANOR CRIES HERSELF TO SLEEP
>ELEANOR SLEEPS HERE …
>
>ONE MORE PUFF AND THEN I'LL JUMP.
>I'LL DEFINITELY, DEFINITELY …
> *Je t'aime et je t'adore.*

(She takes one last drag and prepares to leap off the wing. Amelia, however, suddenly stands up, breaks the boundaries of the plane, and steps out onto the wing.)

AMELIA.
> Miss Hickok, I must ask you to come back inside.

HICK. *(Not noticing Amelia.)*
>THIS IS THE BEGINNING OF A NEW ERA
>IN HUMAN FLIGHT … Watch:

(She realizes Amelia is on the wing.)
> Who's piloting the plane?

AMELIA.
> You shouldn't be jealous.

HICK. *(Facing her down.)*
>JEALOUS OF YOU?
>YOU?
>YOU WITH ALL OF THE HYPE
>AND THE HUSBAND WHO'S IN CHARGE

OF YOUR EVERY MOVE?
Jealous of you?
GIRL, YOU'RE A TRAINED MONKEY.

AMELIA.
Well.... Fine. But I meant that you shouldn't be jealous of my friendship with Eleanor.
SHE HAS A CRUSH ON ME.
IT'S SORT OF SWEET.

HICK. *(Like a threat.)*
Uh-huh.

AMELIA.
I RESPECT YOU.
YOU MADE YOURSELF.
You're lucky that you don't have to hawk toothpaste and gum and "functional clothes."
... YOU'VE DONE A LOT IN YOUR LIFE.

HICK.
My life is going to a Baptist church one Sunday morning down in Atlanta and not having a veil ... and Eleanor tying a napkin to my head and my following her into church.
MY LIFE IS WEARING A NAPKIN
ON MY HEAD AND FOLLOWING ELEANOR.

AMELIA.
Come inside.

HICK.
Why? She doesn't need me to listen to her bad jokes or hand her candy or tell her her hair is a mess.

AMELIA.
SHE NEVER LOOKS INTO A MIRROR.
GREAT LADIES NEVER DO.
SHE NEVER LEARNED TO PRIMP AND PREEN;

SHE NEVER WANTED TO.
SHE'S NEVER EVER FOUND AT HOME.
HER HUSBAND DOESN'T MIND.
HE KNOWS SHE'S DUCKING INTO DUSTBOWL SHACKS
OR DANCING WITH THE BLIND.
SHE NEVER LOOKS INTO A MIRROR.
GREAT LADIES AREN'T VAIN.
SOMEHOW SHE STAYS TOASTY-DRY
IN SPITE OF CONSTANT RAIN.

ELEANOR.   *(From within the plane.)*
... I'm absolutely convinced that there is a future in commercial flight. If handled correctly. Yes, Amelia?

AMELIA.   *(To Eleanor.)*
Yes.
(To Hick.)
SOME WOMEN FEEL THEY CAN FLY OVER OCEANS.
I DO.
SOME WOMEN FEEL LIKE THEY'RE LOST OVER OCEANS.
SOMETIMES
I DO.
THIS WOMAN CROSSES OCEANS
NO ONE'S EVER CROSSED BEFORE.
WHEN YOU GIVE YOUR BEST TO HER
SHE TURNS IT INTO MORE
SO THAT OTHERS: LADIES, WOMEN, PEOPLE,
SO THAT PEOPLE CAN HAVE MORE ...
SHE NEVER GLANCES AT A CLOCK.
GREAT HEROES AREN'T LATE.
SHE WAKES TO SCRAMBLED EGGS AND TROUBLES
HEAPED UPON HER BREAKFAST PLATE.
SHE NEVER LOOKS INTO A MIRROR.
GREAT HEROES NEVER DO.
WHEN SHE NEEDS TO SEE HERSELF
SHE WILL LOOK AT YOU.

You know, there's probably a half-dozen female fliers just as good as me — or better. My husband doesn't like the public to know that.... So.... But.... Her. She's a work of art.

ELEANOR. *(From the plane.)*
LOOK AT WASHINGTON! THAT BRILLIANT GLOW!

HICK.
Dingy. It's dingy. She's not finished yet ...

AMELIA.
Come inside.
(She takes Hick's arm, and leads her back to the plane.)

HICK.
Oh, Miss Earhart, you should tell your husband you want to can the fashion line, the toothpaste and the gum. Tell him you need to fly around the world.
(Amelia smiles, kisses Hick. Hick and Amelia re-enter the tiny plane, Amelia to her seat, Hick to her original squatting place in the back, facing front.)
And you should fly over the Capitol, Eleanor.

ELEANOR.
What?

HICK.
You don't need Franklin's permission, and you don't need mine. It's your life. Fly the aeroplane. Amelia will show you.
(To herself.)
HEADLINE:
"FIRST FIRST LADY TO FLY.
PROVES ... A MULTITUDE OF THINGS."

ELEANOR.
May I, Amelia?

AMELIA.
Here ... take this.... Now: Hold steady ...

ELEANOR. *(Taking the controls.)*
>Look at me! I'm a pilot!
EXTRAORDINARY!
FRANKLIN WILL BE ANGRY.
Look Hick! I'm flying! See?
YOU'RE A WITNESS!
See!

HICK. *(Looking not at Eleanor, but out to the audience. She sees the past, the future — all in one; sad and painful. She accepts it.)*
>I SEE.
I SEE ...
I SEE...!

THE END

PROPERTY LIST

Roll of Lifesaver candies (HICK)
Cigar and lighter (HICK)

SCENE DESIGN
"FIRST LADY SUITE" – 'OVER TEXAS'
(DESIGNED BY DEREK McLANE FOR THE NEW YORK SHAKESPEARE FESTIVAL)

SCENE DESIGN
"FIRST LADY SUITE" – "WHERE'S MAMIE?"
(DESIGNED BY DEREK McLANE FOR THE NEW YORK SHAKESPEARE FESTIVAL)

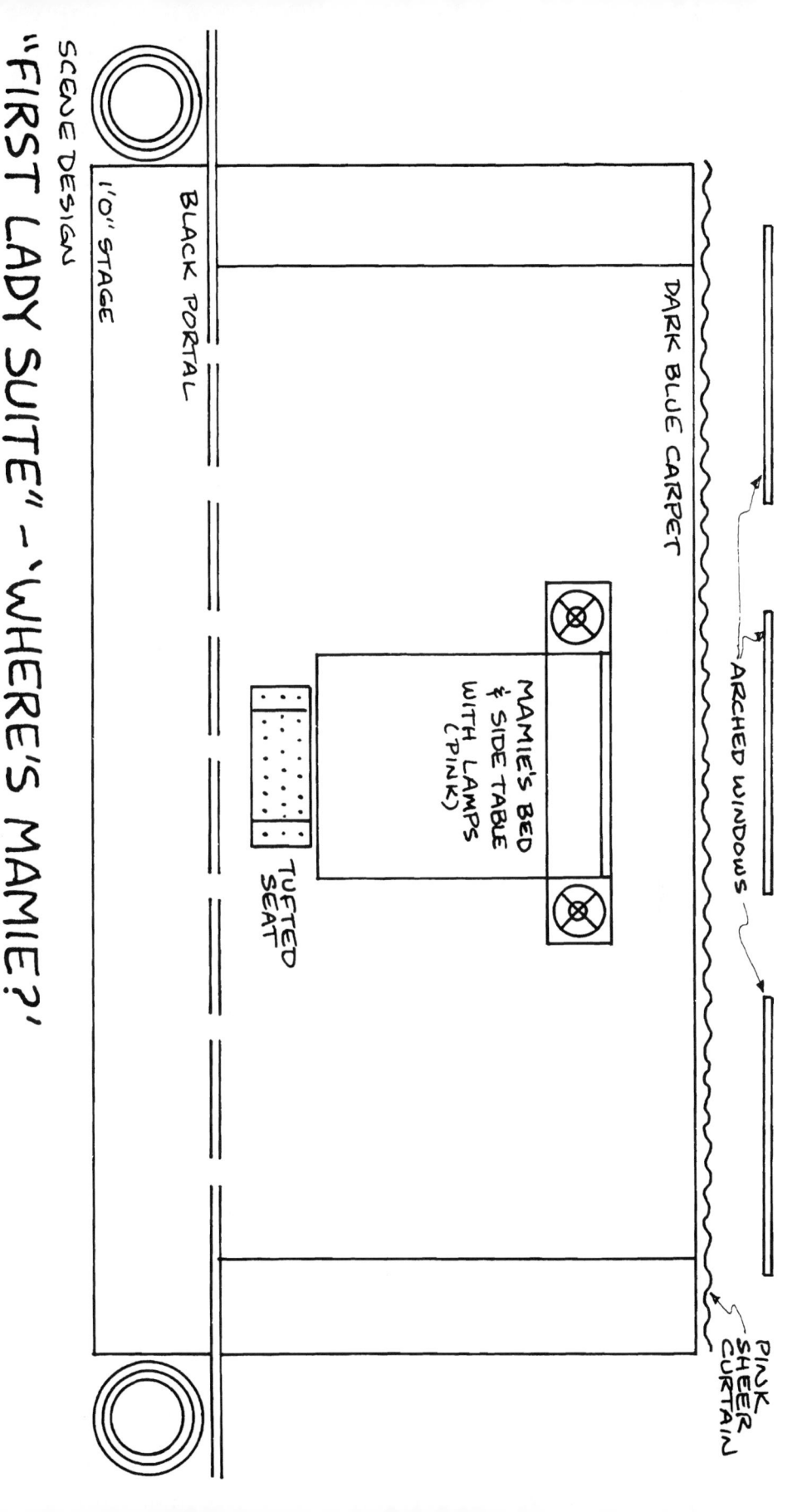

1'0" STAGE
BLACK PORTAL
DARK BLUE CARPET
MAMIE'S BED & SIDE TABLE WITH LAMPS (PINK)
TUFTED SEAT
ARCHED WINDOWS
PINK SHEER CURTAIN

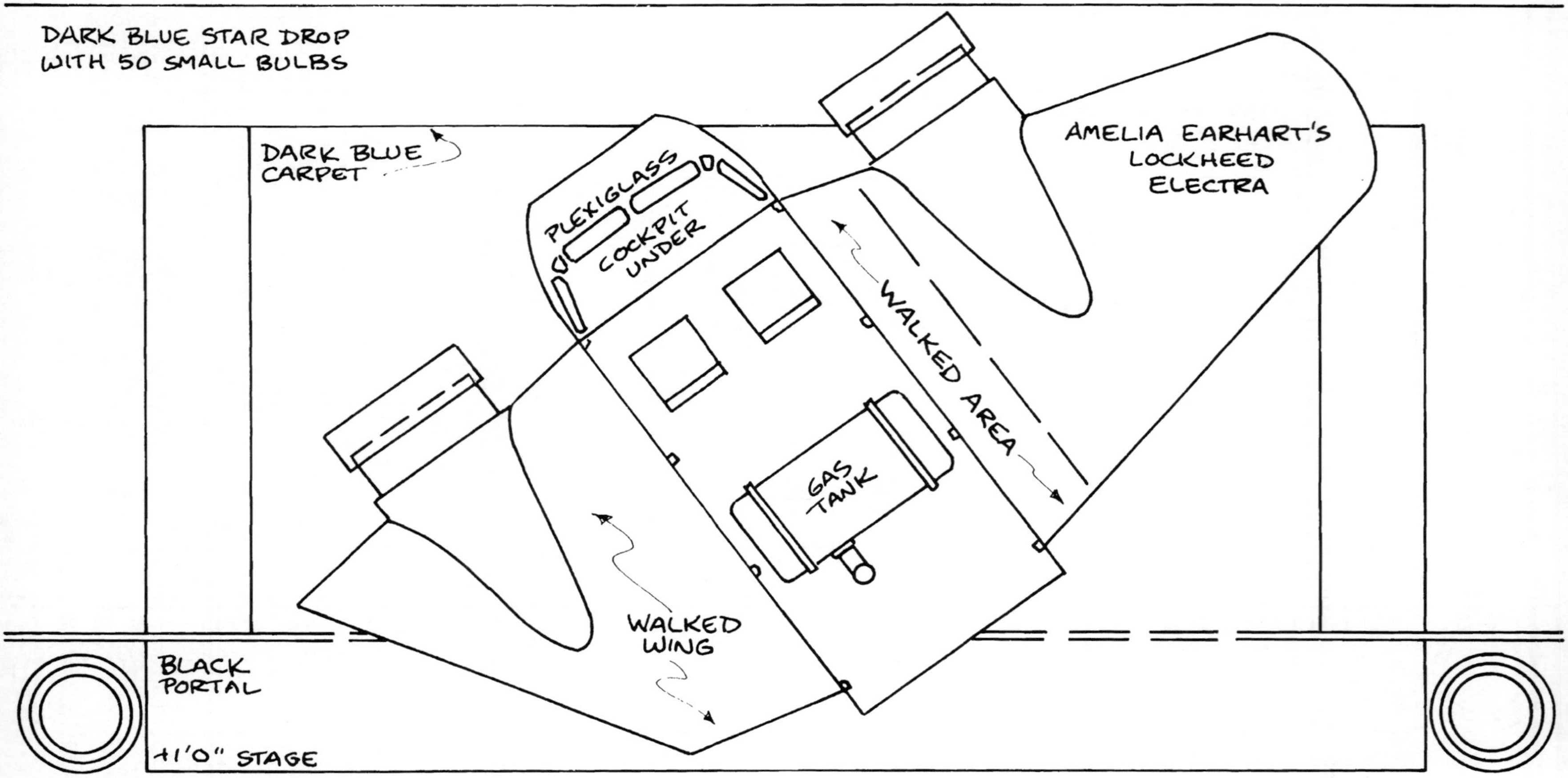

SCENE DESIGN

"FIRST LADY SUITE"–'ELEANOR SLEEPS HERE'

(DESIGNED BY DEREK McLANE FOR THE NEW YORK SHAKESPEARE FESTIVAL)